With a Song in My Heart
The Biography of Stevie Wonder

Kathleen Wiseman and Charles Hirsch

Contents

Rigby
A Harcourt Achieve Imprint

www.Rigby.com
1-800-531-5015

The Talented Stevie Wonder

Who is Stevie Wonder? He has been called a musical genius by many people. By the time he was ten years old, Stevie Wonder could play several musical instruments. He also had a wonderful singing voice. He was so talented that by the age of 13, he had made a hit record album. Stevie was known as "the little boy wonder" because of his gift for music and singing at such a young age.

As Stevie grew up, he wrote most of his own songs and won many awards for his music. Stevie played pop and rock songs as well as jazz, which is a kind of music played with a piano, drums, bass, and trumpet. He also sang gospel, or religious, songs. Today, Stevie still continues to sing and make music.

In addition to making music, Stevie Wonder spends his time helping people. He has raised money to help find cures for diseases and to fight hunger. He also supports people who, due to conditions such as blindness, have special needs. Stevie Wonder truly is wonderful, but how did he get his musical talent and giving heart?

Blind at Birth

Stevie Wonder was born on May 13, 1950, in Saginaw, Michigan. His mother, Lula Mae Hardaway, named him Steveland when he was born. But Baby Stevie's first days after birth were very hard. Because he was born too early, he was very little and his eyes did not have a chance to grow normally.

Baby Stevie was so little that he had to spend many days in an incubator, a special machine that kept him warm and gave him oxygen. However, the incubator gave him too much oxygen. This extra oxygen and his eye problem caused him to become blind. Baby Stevie would never be able to see the world around him.

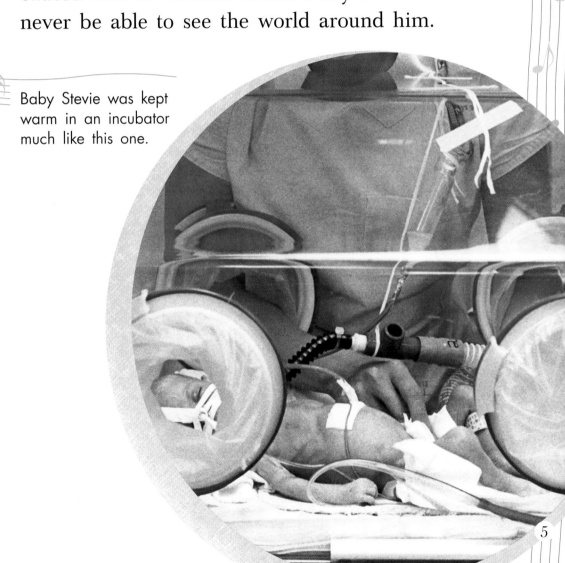

Baby Stevie was kept warm in an incubator much like this one.

The Beat Goes On

Stevie's first few years were spent in Saginaw, Michigan. Then, in 1954, Stevie's mother moved her family to Detroit. When Stevie first moved into his family's new apartment in Detroit, his mother worried about his safety. Because of this, Stevie spent a lot of time indoors, listening to music on the radio. He would also bang spoons on pots and pans to the beat of the music. At a very early age, Stevie had found his love for music!

Welcome to the city of **Detroit**

It was here in Detroit that the world of music opened up to Stevie. He was given a harmonica as a gift. Neighbors also gave him an old piano and a set of bongos, which are a small set of drums played with the hands. A local club even gave Stevie a drum set! He played his instruments constantly, getting better and better.

By the age of nine, Stevie knew how to play the harmonica.

For the Record

At five years of age, Stevie got his first paying job. Band members paid the young musician two quarters for tapping out rhythms with spoons as they played at a picnic.

Music to His Ears

Stevie spent his childhood days riding his bike, playing games, and climbing trees. But music always had a very special place in his life. Stevie could often be found playing the bongos on his front porch. He also loved to have a small radio with him so that he could listen to jazz and other kinds of music.

Stevie practiced singing and playing his instruments with his friends, too. One day, a man named Ronnie White saw Stevie performing. Ronnie was in a very popular band and knew that Stevie had a lot of talent. He wanted to help Stevie become a star!

Ronnie White played with a band called The Miracles.

The Rest Is Music History

Ronnie helped introduce Stevie to Detroit's most famous record company, Motown Records. The name "Motown" actually comes from "Motortown," which is the nickname for Detroit. It's called "Motortown" because many cars and trucks are built in Detroit.

This building is the original recording studio for Motown Records.

Stevie put on a lively show when he met the president of Motown Records. Stevie played his bongos and harmonica, and he sang his very best. Stevie was only ten years old, but the president of the company loved the show so much that he wanted Stevie to make a record album.

The president of Motown Records was amazed at how well Stevie could sing and play harmonica.

The Boy Is a Wonder!

By the time Stevie was 11 years old, he was working on his album with Motown Records. Everyone at Motown loved Stevie because of his positive attitude and sense of humor. When they watched Stevie sing and dance, they thought he was some kind of "wonder" because he was so full of energy. Soon Stevie was known as Little Stevie Wonder.

Stevie performed with many other artists who recorded at Motown.

In 1963, Stevie's album *Little Stevie Wonder, the 12-Year-Old Genius* came out. The album had a hit song called "Fingertips." Little Stevie was now a big star!

All throughout high school, Stevie kept making music and studying his school work. He graduated in 1968 from the Michigan School for the Blind. But Stevie wasn't little anymore. He had grown up and was now known as Stevie Wonder.

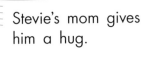

Stevie's mom gives him a hug.

Mind Full of Music

By the time Stevie was 20 years old, he had been making music with Motown for many years. He wrote most of his own songs, he played every instrument, and he made his own records, too! Stevie was a one-man band in the recording studio. However, Stevie wanted to start exploring new sounds and making different kinds of music.

Stevie Wonder's an expert in the recording studio!

When Stevie turned 21 in 1971, his record deal with Motown ended. Stevie was ready for his music to take a new direction! He built his own recording studio. He also moved to New York City where he discovered a special electronic instrument called a synthesizer, which is often played with a keyboard. With a synthesizer, Stevie could create sounds in his music that he'd never been able to do before. He recorded songs with these new sounds on an album called *Music of My Mind.*

Stevie's music continued to change and grow after his album *Music of My Mind*. In 1972, he released a new album called *Talking Book*. With this album, Stevie did something very special for his fans that were blind. The first covers of *Talking Book* were printed in Braille, which is a special kind of writing and printing system for people who are blind. Braille uses raised dots that stand for letters and numbers.

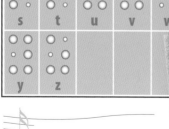

Braille alphabet

For the Record

Stevie's message in Braille read: "Here is my music. It is all that I have to tell you how I feel. Know that your love keeps my love strong.

—Stevie"

STEVIE WONDER

TALKING BOOK

Stevie's music on *Talking Book* was very popular and he won several awards for this album. He was even asked to perform a hit song from his album on the children's television show *Sesame Street*! People of all ages loved Stevie's music.

Stevie attended many award ceremonies for his album.

That's What Friends Are For

After the album *Talking Book* was released, Stevie continued to make award-winning music. He began to work with other musical recording artists, too. In 1972, he went on tour with a band called the Rolling Stones. Stevie even traveled to Jamaica in 1975 to play a concert with Bob Marley and the Wailers. The concert raised money for a special school for the blind.

Stevie toured with bands such as the Rolling Stones.

In the 1980s, Stevie still made music with his friends. Stevie co-wrote songs and played music with Paul McCartney. Stevie and Paul sang a song together called "Ebony and Ivory." Stevie also worked with his friends Dionne Warwick, Gladys Knight, and Elton John to create the award-winning song, "That's What Friends Are For."

Stevie and Paul McCartney played a musical instrument called a cabasa.

While Stevie made music, he still found time to use his music to support world peace and end hunger. Stevie even wrote a song called "Happy Birthday" in honor of Dr. Martin Luther King, Jr. and worked with many others to make Dr. Martin Luther King's birthday a national holiday. Stevie hoped that this holiday would help continue Dr. King's dream of love and peace among all people.

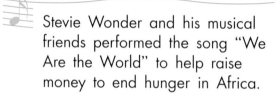

Stevie Wonder and his musical friends performed the song "We Are the World" to help raise money to end hunger in Africa.

Stevie also helped make a book for children. He worked with an author on the book *Little Stevie Wonder in Places Under the Sun.* This book is very special because it has both Braille and printed text together so that all readers can enjoy the story!

Braille books let children who are blind read the same books as children who can see.

High Notes

Stevie has been given many awards for all the great things he's done in his life. In 1989, Stevie was awarded for his musical ability. He was given a place in the Rock and Roll Hall of Fame, which is a museum that honors talented rock and roll musicians.

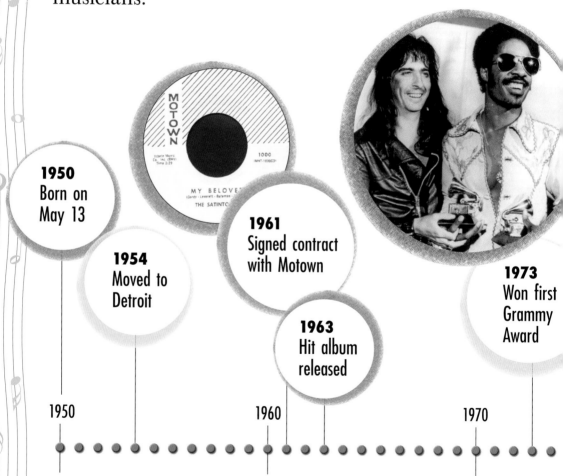

1950
Born on May 13

1954
Moved to Detroit

1961
Signed contract with Motown

1963
Hit album released

1973
Won first Grammy Award

1950   1960   1970

On December 5, 1999, Stevie received the Kennedy Center Honor. This award is given to people who have been very successful as singers, musicians, dancers, actors, or comedians. In 2002, the Songwriters Hall of Fame gave Stevie an award for his musical success throughout his life. Stevie has also received many other awards for the time he's spent helping others.

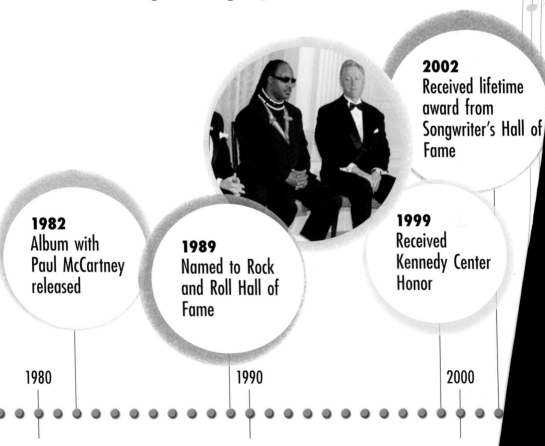

2002
Received lifetime award from Songwriter's Hall of Fame

1982
Album with Paul McCartney released

1989
Named to Rock and Roll Hall of Fame

1999
Received Kennedy Center Honor

1980

1990

2000

Today, Stevie Wonder still writes songs, plays music, and helps people in need. He also shares his message about staying positive. Stevie has said, "Just because a man lacks the use of his eyes doesn't mean he lacks vision." Through his music and his words, Stevie has shown us how he sees the world through his eyes.